ENDO

WHY WORSHIP?

AN AWAKENING TO THE
POWER OF PRAISE

HEATHER
LUCIER

LIFEWISE BOOKS

WHY WORSHIP?
AN AWAKENING TO THE POWER OF PRAISE

BY HEATHER LUCIER

Published by:

 LIFEWISE BOOKS

PO BOX 1072
Pinehurst, TX 77362
LifeWiseBooks.com

Cover Design and Interior Layout | Yvonne Parks | PearCreative.ca

To contact the author:
ReviverMinistries.com

ISBN (Print): 978-1-947279-24-7
ISBN (Ebook): 978-1-947279-25-4

Printed and bound in Canada

DEDICATION

I dedicate this book to Ethan.

Who is Ethan? Good question. Ethan was the little
five-year-old boy who made me crazy with all his
questions. He used to follow me around the church,
asking why I was doing whatever it was I was doing.
Of course, each answer I gave would only lead to the
next question —"why?"

When I confronted him one day and asked why he
asked so many questions, he defiantly put his little
hands on his hips and said quite pointedly, "'Cause I
need to know stuff!"

What annoyed me then, I admire today so many
years later. We need to ask questions. If we don't ask,
we won't know. And if we don't know, how can we
succeed?

So, thank you, Ethan, for all your questions, and
I hope this book will provide you with an answer
should you ever ask the question:

Why worship?

– Heather Lucier

TABLE OF CONTENTS

ACKNOWLEDGEMENTS
In Acknowledgement of My Two Greatest Promoters...

My father, the late Samuel Alfred Bowen:

There are three words that are not used in this day and age as much as they should be. But if I had to describe my father with only three words, they would be: integrity, righteousness and honour.

He was dedicated to his wife for 57 years, served his God faithfully, always kept his word, and loved his family dearly. He wanted more for others than he did for himself. He often said to me "I will bend over backwards to help you" and indeed he did.

Although he was a man of few words, he spoke more into my life by how he lived committed to the Word of God. I will never forget listening to him pray every night as he knelt at the side of his bed with his Bible open before him. I believe it was the grace of God that took him home in the early morning hours of November 22, 2017 after living on this earth for 85 years and struggling with Parkinson's disease the last few years of his life.

I feel honored to be called his daughter. He was a great man who inspired one of my life's goals of continuing his legacy of righteousness, integrity and honour by knowing and searching the scriptures.

Dad, thank you for showing me how to live in a way that pleases the heart of God. I will miss you.

**My husband, friend and life-companion,
Arthur Charles Lucier:**

I have the distinct privilege and opportunity to live my life with a man who not only loves God but is also passionate about the things of God and worship. He has set a standard of worship most are challenged by, and always strives to go deeper towards the heart of God through worship and praise.

He is an amazing father to our twin sons Jesse and Jayden. I am blessed to travel, play music and worship with these guys, as a family worship team. Our goal is to inspire others to worship wholeheartedly, pleasing our God and King.

Arthur, thank you for your ongoing, support, encouragement and example that you set for me and for others, in this so important area of our walk with God. I love you.

Psalm 86:9

"All the nations you have made will come and worship before you, Lord; they will bring glory to your name."

WORSHIP: "To bow oneself down; to sink down, to be depressed; to depress; to honour; to do homage, to submit oneself."[1]

INTRODUCTION

Growing up, we went to church every Sunday. There were certain routines we adhered to faithfully. As much as I love routine, I have often questioned certain things. I don't know if it is just in my nature to question, but question I do: why do we do what we do?

My "Sunday" always started after dinner Saturday evening—the big ordeal, which would prepare me for my Sunday debut.

It began with my mother, who started to gather what she needed to tame my hair and make me presentable for Sunday morning. The process started with her dragging out the cast-iron comb that she stored in a cloth bag in the bottom drawer of the stove with all of the frying pans. She would unwrap it and place it gently on one of the circular elements of the stove, and then turn the element on high.

Yes, that is correct! I did say "cast-iron comb," and yes, she would heat it up on the stove! Now to most of you non-African Americans, I'm sure this seems somewhat unbelievable to you, but I assure you, the words I pen are true.

Next, Mom would get out the hair grease, the large plastic comb, and some clips, set a tall stool close to the stove, and hoist me on top of the stool. She would partition my hair into small sections, add a bit of grease, and then very carefully, she would take the now red-hot comb and run it slowly through the partitioned section of my hair.

She would warn me every few minutes "Now don't move," and I would hold my breath as I heard the searing sounds and smelled the distasteful odor of hair being singed, as smoke emanated off the comb. Then she would place the comb back on the stove element to re-heat it and move on to the next section of hair.

This was the "straightening" process, which took approximately an hour. Now, when you are a child, an hour might as well be an eternity. Inevitably, I would get bored and start to fidget, and my mom would warn me again, "Don't move!"

It pretty much became routine that my only brother would come running through the kitchen at some point, causing me to turn and look just at the wrong moment. And yes, you guessed it—the comb would graze my flesh, and I would yelp, prompting Mom to proclaim, "I told you not to move!" She would insist that my brother leave the room, and on we would go.

After carefully straightening my hair in this manner, she would then place hard plastic rollers in my hair, securing them with large, unforgiving bobby pins. This was to give my hair some curl, now that we had straightened it, and off to bed I would go.

I'm sure you can imagine how difficult it was to sleep with small burns scattered around the nape of my neck. It was extremely difficult to find that exact position on my pillow that didn't cause the rollers to dent my tender skull or be skewered by a bobby pin. In the morning, the rollers would come out, and my mother would masterfully create a beautiful hair-do for me. She was always quite thrilled with the outcome, but I was only left with a bunch of "why's"?

Why did God give me this hair? Why, since God gave me this hair, could we not just leave it "as is"? Why did I have to get all "done-up" just to go to church? Does God really care what my hair looks like? These were just some of the things I questioned as a child.

Thankfully, the hair straightening process is somewhat less torturous these days, but there are still many things I question about the whole "going to church routine" that we surrender ourselves to. One of them, which this book addresses is: why worship?

Many specialized, detailed books can take you through the history of worship, the impact of worship on the church, styles of worship, perspectives on worship, worship leaders' manuals, and even an exegetical analysis of worship, just to name a few.

This book is not that. It is based on my own experiences in worship; from that place, I explain what I believe worship should be.

The truth is, this book is not meant to be a study, a directive, or an instructive manual about worship, but it might be better described as a "prolonged exhortation to worship."

My heart is to simply answer the question, "Why worship?" My goal is for each of us to understand the heart of God towards worship and ultimately lead us to a place where we can evaluate our worship and go deeper in our own worship before Him.

Psalm 7:17

"I will give thanks to the L<small>ORD</small> *because of his righteousness; I will sing the praises of the name of the* L<small>ORD</small> *Most High."*

PRAISES: "sing; praise; sing, praise; play an instrument"[1]
"…to play on a musical instrument; to sing so accompanied."[2]

CHAPTER 1

THINGS HAVE CHANGED

One of my favorite shows of all time *(now don't laugh)* was *Little House on the Prairie.* To tell the truth, I'm not even sure why. I do know that I loved the innocence of their way of life. In their family unit, "Ma" and "Pa" were clearly in love with each other, and the love flowed down to the children. I'm not an emotionally inclined person, but that was one show that could always bring tears to my eyes. Whenever Charles got teary, I would find myself sniffling right along with him.

What always amazed me about this show, was it didn't seem to matter what was happening, who was having a disagreement, or what anyone was doing at the time—when that little church bell rang, everything stopped while everyone put on their Sunday best, and off to church they went.

The townsfolk would come together, and with united voices, you could hear them singing "Bringing in the Sheaves," or something similar. Somehow, I feel like even in the innocence of this show, they had an understanding about the heart of God in worship.

The truth of the matter is, things have changed. Church bells don't ring much anymore, most of us don't know what "sheaves" are, and nowadays people come to church *if* and *when* they feel like it. Our Sunday best, at least in my neck of the woods, has at times been a semi-clean pair of jeans and a relatively unwrinkled t-shirt, or sweat shirt and a bra if you are lucky. During our long winter months, some come to church in their knee-high snow boots with lounge pants tucked deep inside. One Saturday night, one of my back-up singers came to church in her husband's steel-toed gum boots. I'm sure Caroline Ingalls would turn over in her grave. Truly, the *Little House on the Prairie* days are long gone.

Today, we live in a whole new world. Life is fast paced, and people are busy with their "stuff." We have gone from a God-centered society to a humanistic society. Our world is no longer devoted to God but to self, personal gain, and advancement. We teach "look out for number one," "always watch your back," and "only the best man wins." We live in a world where the supernatural and the divine are confused, and our knowledge of God is superficial at best.

Today, in our modern churches, many do not have an understanding as to why we worship. The concept of worship and praise is foreign to most people, especially those who do not have a church background. Often the churched and un-churched have this idea that the worship service is a time for them to come and be entertained and pumped up with some good music.

The concepts and intention behind the worship and praise we read about in the Bible has often not been taught, and it seems the church has moved farther away from what the scriptures define worship to be, towards an entertainment-oriented, "make me feel-good" mentality.

Whether you are new to the church or have been around since the dark ages, I believe we need a fresh understanding of what the word of God refers to when worship and praise are referenced. So many different definitions are attached to the words "worship" and "praise." We need to understand each one in context so that we have a better picture of what the scriptures' intention is for us.

As nice as it was to watch all the townsfolk of *Little House on the Prairie* come together and sing the old hymns, I don't know that even they understood why they worshipped…or did they?

Psalm 29: 1-2

"Ascribe to the LORD, you heavenly beings, ascribe to the LORD glory and strength. Ascribe to the LORD the glory due his name; worship the LORD in the splendor of his holiness."

WORSHIP: "To prostrate oneself before any one out of honour."[1]

CHAPTER 2

THE "NO TOWN" SOUND

My worship experience has been rather diverse. Having been born under a pew, so to speak, I literally never missed church as a child. We attended church Sunday morning, Sunday evening, and Wednesday evening for prayer because that was just as important. My life revolved around church: church people, church events, special church speakers, church meetings, church potlucks, and my skating class. But even then, church took priority over skating.

I remember all too well my parents picking me up outside the skating arena on Sundays at 6:50pm. Even though my skating class didn't end till 7, we had to be at church by 7 and ready for worship. So, my family would swing by, and I would jump in the back seat of our old Pontiac, with my skates still on. Between there and the three-minute drive up the hill to the church, I had to get the skates off, get out of my skating dress and tights and into my Sunday evening dress, tame my hair, get my shoes on, and be ready to get out of the car when it came to a halt in the church parking lot. All this occurred with my brother sitting next to me, bugging me the whole time.

We would enter our little church, and soon after the pianist or organist would begin to play, we would open our red hymnals and sing some rousing hymns of praise and worship. Occasionally, we would sing from the chorus book, but not too often because choruses were not yet widely accepted. We were Pentecostal, after all, but still somewhat reserved.

It was in that environment that I learned to play the accordion and the piano. I loved to sing and listen to those singing around me, but even then, I remember wondering why it was that some people could be so cranky and miserable just before going into church, and then again right after church, but at the same time sing these beautiful songs of praise and worship to God. As a child, it seemed odd, to say the least. Now, I would probably use the word "hypocritical."

In my early teens, I started playing piano in church for my aunt, who was the main worship leader at the time. She had a unique style, which we affectionately called "the No-town sound", after the "Motown" sound, but I figured it was because there was no other town in the world that sounded like we did.

We would often pack our cars with amplifiers, guitars, and a clunky little keyboard, and head to the little villages in the area, where we would sing and minister to the First Nations people. Now those townsfolk could really sing! Sometimes, we would literally sing the same chorus over and over twenty to thirty times, and no one thought it was strange. No one, that is, except maybe me. All I know is, my fingers would get so sore that inside my head I was yelling, "enough, end the song already!"

From there, my worship experience took a dramatic turn. At seventeen, I left home and moved to Portland, Oregon to attend Portland Bible College. I had no idea what I was in for; I just knew I wanted to get away from the small-town scene.

I will never forget my first worship experience at my new college. I started mid-term in January, instead of September like everyone else, and was one of maybe ten newcomers to the school at that time. They held orientation in the little chapel, as was the custom at the beginning of each new semester. I remember being excited and a bit nervous for this new lease on life. The dean of the school got up and welcomed everyone back to the new semester. He then said,

"All right, let's take ten or so minutes and worship the Lord and pray."

Almost before the words left his lips, the students and faculty alike all began to cry out in loud praise and worship, even though there was no music. Some stood up with their hands lifted high; some left their seats and stood with their faces to the wall calling out to God; others paced back and forth, shouting and declaring. Some were laying on the floor prostrate before God. It all started so suddenly, and was so loud, that it literally scared me.

I slid out of my seat onto my knees and began praying with all my heart. "God what have I done? What is this place? Is this a cult? What am I doing here?" I was so scared, and on the verge of tears, when after about fifteen minutes (although it seemed like an eternity), it stopped, and everyone sat down again, then they quickly moved on to the next order of business.

I later became accustomed to that style of spontaneous worship and prayer and really enjoyed it. It was so energetic. The unity in the room brought the presence of God so quickly. Sometimes there was a piano playing, but the music was inconsequential. It was the united voices in single-minded focus, giving God loud, uninhibited, glorious praise, that always electrified the room.

I had gone to college to study music and came away with so much more. The college was part of a church called Bible Temple (now City Bible Church), and at the time it housed over a thousand people. The music department was phenomenal—it was not just the little pianist and organist anymore. They housed a full orchestra, with trumpets, trombones, flutes, violins, and even a harpist.

The music was professional and well done. We would sing the newest songs of praise and worship, and there was always room for the spontaneous songs of the Lord and the prophetic word. It was so different from where I had come from. I felt like everything I knew about God and worship was obsolete, and I was on this incredible new adventure to learn what worship really was.

After college, I came home and got married. Our lives took us to several different churches, some non-denominational, some Pentecostal, some Vineyard. Each had its own style and flair for worship. Often, my husband and I would be part of the worship team or in some cases, we *were* the worship team. It seemed the smaller churches always had a need for musicians and singers, and because my husband and I could do both...well, you can guess what happened.

At one church we attended, the pastor asked my husband Art and I to be the worship leaders. This caused resentment among some members of the congregation because we were replacing the old pianist, who had been there for quite some time. It's somewhat difficult to lead people into worship when their eyes are glaring at you just above their chorus books.

In that particular scenario, we were displaced when someone better came along, but then quickly reinstated when they only lasted a month or so (this happened a few times in the course of 18 months). It all seems a bit comical now, but at the time, it was quite hurtful and confusing. Of course, I can now see the hand of God in it, because it was in those difficult and humbling times that we learned to stand strong, and our character was forged in the fires of adversity.

Even with all of these varying experiences, I still deep down inside question whether we, the church, really know what true worship is. I'm talking about the type of worship that King David, even before he was king, gave to God—the type of worship that caught God's attention and made the angels stop just for a second to give a listen and nod their approval. That's the kind of worship I seek after—the kind of worship that captures the attention of the one I love.

Psalm 9:1-2

*"I will give thanks to you, L*ORD*, with all my heart; I will tell of all your wonderful deeds. I will be glad and rejoice in you; I will sing the praises of your name, O Most High."*

PRAISES: "sing praises; play notes on instrument"[1]

CHAPTER 3
A WORSHIP LEADER'S PERSPECTIVE

As a worship leader and pastor who also does itinerate worship ministry, I have the unique advantage of watching people worship. After all, I'm up on the platform looking out over the congregation. Unless I close my eyes the entire time (which I sometimes want to do if I don't like what I see), I get to see people engage...or not...in worship.

Over the years I've seen the "obligated worshippers." These are the ones who are in worship out of obligation. The husband or the wife has dragged them there. It's impossible for them to hide it. They look less than amused...bored really. They may be fiddling around, adjusting a chair, checking their cell phone, digging in their purse, straightening their child's hair, looking around to see if something in the room is more interesting than what is happening in worship. They stand, then sit, then sprawl. Sometimes they will engage for a moment if a familiar song is sung, but other than that, they just are not really there.

Then there are the "strained worshippers." These are ones to whom it seems worship is difficult, or maybe even painful for them. They position themselves and often don't move at all during the entire worship time. Some hide their faces in their hands. Some recline their heads back on their seats, with eyes closed and brows painfully furrowed, and almost appear to be sleeping. If I should ask for everyone to stand, you can visibly see that it is a great effort for them to rise, and once standing, they seem confused and a bit lost. Sometimes it appears that they want to engage, and that indeed something may be happening inside them, but the whole process seems a difficult endeavor for them.

Of course, there are the "up and down worshippers." These are the most interesting to watch. When the music begins, they stand and sing along with everyone else, and they may even raise their hands; but then before the first song is over, they leave their seat and go….? Then, almost as suddenly as they left, they are back again and quickly engaged, but not before stopping to give the wife a quick kiss on the cheek because…? Suddenly, they grab their phone, and away they go to the back to make a mysterious phone call. Once again, they come in, look around to see where we are in worship, join in and sing a line or two, then suddenly grab their jacket and out they go again! Usually, they make it back in time for the last song and seem somehow pleased and satisfied that they did their worship duty for the week.

Then there are the "young-mom worshippers." I admire these women. They deserve notoriety, attention, applause, and a badge of honor. Being a mother of twin boys, I remember the days and understand all too well what it is like trying to get your worship on when you have toddlers literally pulling your pants down while your hands are lifted in worship to God. Trying to teach your children to worship with all their little hearts is so beautiful and important. It does, however, pose a difficult—nay, a dangerous situation, when your little one wants to flag during worship and is adamant that whacking others with sticks is the ultimate form of praise to God.

Of course, there are the "beautiful worshippers." These come in coiffed and combed and sit very neatly. They would raise their hands all the way, but that might cause their shirt to wrinkle or rise up, so it is better for them to raise their arms from the elbows only. Dramatic demonstrations in worship are a concern for them because it seems disorderly and unkempt. And dancing in church? Oh my, that would mess up the hair and the well-thought-out ensemble they are wearing—nonsense! After all, is not everything to be done "decently and in order?"

Then there are the "feeler worshippers." These are always a surprise. It's kind of like opening the cereal box and never knowing what the prize is going to be at the bottom. The feelers are often the best worshippers, depending, however, on how they feel.

When the feelers are engaged, they have the ability to shift the spiritual atmosphere in the room so quickly, because they worship will all their hearts. When they feel the presence of God come, it energizes them, and they worship with amazing abandonment. But unfortunately, the feelers also have the power to squelch things in the spirit, if the feeler's feelings are feeling off.

We can't forget in this day and age the "cell phone worshippers." This is pretty much self-explanatory. These ones are always careful to position their phones just within their peripheral vision so that they can give the phone a quick cursory glance every so often as they worship, so as not to miss any notifications. If such an incident should occur, they have the unique ability to disengage from worship, check their notification, and maybe even peck out a quick response before quickly reengaging within seconds. What can I say?

Then there are the "wanting worshippers." These are my personal favorite as a worship leader. They simply love to worship and want more. They engage from the beginning and are focused no matter what the song is, who is singing it, or what is going on around them. You can see they are focused in on the one they have come to worship—the one they love. They are not afraid to display their love and affection for the Lord, no matter what it looks like. These are the ones who give me the desire to keep doing what I do and inspire me to give it my all.

Now, should anyone be offended with my synopsis, you must understand that I am not judging. It's simply my observation. I have toyed with the idea that it would be great if the worship leader and team could turn around and not face the congregation; this way it would be easier to not see what is happening out in the crowd. I do wish that everyone had the opportunity to lead and see congregational worship from the worship leader's perspective. I propose that some would change their worship style if they could see themselves through this unique lens. But still, the question remains: is this true worship? And why are we doing it anyway?

Psalm 100:1-2

"Shout for joy to the Lord all the earth. Worship the Lord with gladness; come before him with joyful song."

WORSHIP: "To labour, to work; to do work; to serve, to work, to worship, to serve Jehovah with anything" [1]

CHAPTER 4

SO, WHAT IS WORSHIP ANYWAY?

The subject of worship can be overwhelming at best. It can be approached from so many different angles that it's difficult to know what to say about it. Having been a music major during my Bible college years, I have read many books, and still, occasionally read something that brings a renewed understanding of the topic to my heart.

When I use the word "worship" in this book, I'm talking about our most common, modern-day expression of worship and praise in the North American church today. I realize that, depending on where you live in this great world of ours, your experience may differ from mine. I have had the opportunity to experience a few other cultures in worship, and it is clear that what I see on this side of the globe would not apply. I have been to some remote places in Africa and

South America where it seems there is a deeper, more resonant understanding of what worship is meant to be. However, for the sake of this book, I would say that I am mostly referring to worship as singing in a corporate church setting, with the accompaniment of music.

Yes, it is true, not all worship is singing as Romans 12:1 so aptly states.

> *"Therefore, I urge you, brothers and sisters, in view of God's mercy, to offer your bodies as a living sacrifice, holy and pleasing to God—this is your true and proper 'worship.'"*

The word "worship" here is defined as "ministry, religious service, duties."[2] This scripture does not speak about or imply worship in the sense of singing or music. Paul is exhorting the Roman church to offer themselves, their whole lives, in righteous living to God as their worship. In my mind, this is unequivocally the highest form of worship and indeed a requirement for us even today. All that we do, indeed our entire lives, should be worship unto God.

It is also true that not all worship requires music, as we see in the story of Jesus dialoguing with the woman at the well in John 4:21-24:

"'Woman,' Jesus replied, 'believe me, a time is coming when you will worship the Father neither on this mountain nor in Jerusalem. You Samaritans worship what you do not know; we worship what we do know, for salvation is from the Jews. Yet a time is coming and has now come when the true worshipers will worship the Father in the Spirit and in truth, for they are the kind of worshipers the Father seeks. God is spirit, and his worshipers must worship in the Spirit and in truth.'"

The word worship in this text means "to bow down, to prostrate oneself before, to worship; to do reverence, to kneel down."[3] The worshipers bow down as a sign of adoration and reverence. The word "Spirit" can be translated as "Holy Spirit, wind, breath, inner being, or way of thinking."[4] "Truth" defined here is "truth, sincerity, integrity, faithfulness, authentic, genuine, etc."[5] I love how the Amplified Translation puts it:

"Jesus replied, 'Woman, believe Me, a time is coming [when God's kingdom comes] when you will worship the Father neither on this mountain nor in Jerusalem. You [Samaritans] do not know what you worship; we [Jews] do know what we worship, for salvation is from the Jews. But a time is coming and is already here when the true worshipers will worship the Father in

spirit [from the heart, the inner self] and in truth; for
the Father seeks such people to be His worshipers. God
is spirit [the Source of life, yet invisible to mankind],
and those who worship Him must worship in spirit
and truth."⁶

In this passage of scripture, the worship described is not about the music. "But a time is coming and is already here when the true worshipers will worship the Father in spirit (from the heart and inner self)." Indeed, a time is coming when true worshippers will bow their hearts, realizing that there is only one true God. A coming awakening through Holy Spirit will bring an understanding of who God is, and mankind will bow in reverence before him.

Worship is a matter of the heart. It's a realization of the fact that there is a God who not only created us and loves us, but, by virtue of who He is, demands a reverence and a surrender of our heart, mind, and will towards him. When we have this revelation, it is so easy and desirable to give him homage and praise. This awareness aligns our hearts to God's purposes and brings an overwhelming joy and desire to express our love to and for him.

Too many people have the notion that worship is about them. I have had people say to me "I just don't get anything out of the worship service; I just like the preaching time." In reality, these people do not understand what worship is. It's not about the music or lack thereof; it's not about a particular style of song; and it's not about what we can get out of it. It's about giving to God what He deserves—it's about honoring him with our whole heart!

This is the longing that drives me. It is the thing that makes me want to shout to God, to dance before Him, to sing as loudly as I can to Him. My heart longs to give Him "my everything" in my display of worship.

Psalm 95:6

"Come, let us bow down in worship, let us kneel before the Lord our Maker; for he is our God and we are the people of his pasture, the flock under his care."

WORSHIP: "To bend one's knee; to bow down; to kneel down; to break down; to cause to bow down.[1]

CHAPTER 5
THE DAVIDIC STANDARD: HUMILITY

When I read John 4:24, quoted in the previous chapter, I can see this same longing of the heart in the Psalms that David wrote. David was a friend of God. No other person in history obtained the endorsement from God that David did when God said of him, "he is a man after my own heart." What was it about David that made God say that of him? After all, we can read his story, and even though he did some mighty things, he also made some major mistakes in his life. Is it possible that it's not what we do or what we have accomplished that draws the heart of God to us? Is it not our heart's longing towards Him that draws Him closer to us?

I love the story of David bringing the Ark of the Covenant back to the City of David from Obed-Edom's house.

After much war and destruction David desires for the Ark of the Covenant to come to the City of David. His first attempt fails miserably and causes the death of Uzziah, one of the priests, because in his zeal, he does not heed God's instructions. David drops the ark off at Obed-Edom's house and goes home, somewhat defeated. After David gets over himself, he makes another attempt to bring the ark home. This time, however, he is much more careful in following the instructions of God. (Selah)

The story is told in 2 Samuel 6:12-16.

> *"Now King David was told, 'The LORD has blessed the household of Obed-Edom and everything he has, because of the ark of God.' So David went to bring up the ark of God from the house of Obed-Edom to the City of David with rejoicing. When those who were carrying the ark of the LORD had taken six steps, he sacrificed a bull and a fattened calf. Wearing a linen ephod, David was dancing before the LORD with all his might, while he and all Israel were bringing up the ark of the LORD with shouts and the sound of trumpets.*

The scripture says that David, wearing a linen ephod, was dancing. Why was it pointed out what he was wearing? I believe the significance is that David, even though he was King, did not think himself too mighty or important to humble himself, take off the constraints of his position, and openly display his heart of rejoicing and thankfulness to God and those around him. If only we could catch this heart today in our worship services. Too many of us are concerned about what others might "think" if we were to truly "let it all hang out" so to speak.

I had a discussion with a gentleman in our church not too long ago about this very thing. I have watched this person worship over the years and I can see a warrior spirit in him. At times I've felt he's wanted to break-out and just let loose in his worship. Once, I did see him in the back "semi-dancing," but he was obviously self-conscious about it. I told him after the service that he should just let loose; that his worship, although constrained, had inspired me. He openly admitted it was pride that was holding him back. I do appreciate his honesty and insight into his own heart, but as a worship leader, it makes me want to scream when I hear that!

We must get over ourselves in worship! God turned his face to David because David gave his *all* to God. Our worship should do the same; it should, in a sense, demand God's presence. Our personal pride will absolutely and always hinder this! I believe more of us need to strip off the constraints of our positions and openly display our worship to God.

God doesn't care if you can dance like the next person. He doesn't care about how good your voice is, and He is most certainly not concerned how your hair looks or how neatly pressed your suit jacket is. He could not care less about whether you forgot to put deodorant on today, and He doesn't even care if parts of your body flop or jiggle when you move. These are literally some of the excuses I have heard from people who are "afraid" to display their worship.

God doesn't care about any of that. His concern is for humility and passion from the heart! Humility is what God loves and what He cannot ignore.

Psalm 22:22-23

"I will declare your name to my people; in the assembly I will praise you. You who fear the Lord, praise Him! All you descendants of Jacob, honor him! Revere him, all you descendants of Israel!"

PRAISE: "to make a show; to be foolish; to sing; to praise; to celebrate."[1]

CHAPTER 6

THE DAVIDIC STANDARD: INSPIRED OR DESPISED

Another point of interest in this story is that King David's worship had one of two effects on those who witnessed it: it either inspired others to join in or caused him to be despised. Somehow, I feel that the same should be said of our worship today. Does your worship inspire others to worship?

> *"...while he and all Israel were bringing up the Ark of the Lord with shouts and the sounds of the trumpet."*[2]

The implication is that everyone joined in worshiping with David. I don't think there were a lot of spectators on the scene. Those who saw David and the dancers were inspired and joined in. His worship drew others into the moment, and inspired them to worship. This is what our worship should do. Does your worship inspire others to join in? It is not just the worship leader's job to encourage people to engage in worship—it is the job of everyone!

It is my opinion that your job, as you worship, is to provoke others to worship. You should worship in such a way that others want to join in, just as in the story of David. Don't ever think that your job is simply to come to church, sit in the worship service, and give a mediocre display of affection to God. Your worship, or the lack thereof, affects the person sitting beside you. It affects the spiritual atmosphere of the worship service. It also sends a message to the next generation about what is okay to do or not do in worship. Most importantly, it either attracts or discourages the heart of God.

I have jokingly used the expression with my children, "do as I say, not as I do." The truth of the matter is, our children will do what they see us do, no matter what we say. I have watched families bring up their children in church, and you can always tell which kids have parents who worship and which ones don't. Kids tend to do what their parents do. I have watched many parents tell their kids, without words, that worship is not important. They may not mean to, but the message is coming through loud and clear.

My husband and I have always been acutely aware that our kids are watching every move we make. When I worship, I want to provoke my children to worship. I want to draw them and others toward God, just as David's worship did.

When there is unity in worship, there a commanded presence. God loves unity, and He loves worship. Imagine the powerful presence of God that would come if every Christian in all churches across North America worshipped with uninhibited abandonment as David did. The face of our churches would look so different than they do now.

The flip side to this story is that King David's worship was so impassioned and so raw, his own wife despised his display of affection.

> *"As the ark of the LORD was entering the City of David, Michal daughter of Saul watched from a window. And when she saw King David leaping and dancing before the LORD, she despised him in her heart…*
>
> *When David returned home to bless his household, Michal daughter of Saul came out to meet him and said, 'How the king of Israel has distinguished himself today, going around half-naked in full view of the slave girls of his servants as any vulgar fellow would.'*

David said to Michal, 'It was before the LORD, who chose me rather than your father or anyone from his house when he appointed me ruler over the LORD's people Israel—I will celebrate before the LORD. I will become even more undignified than this, and I will be humiliated in my own eyes. But by these slave girls you spoke of, I will be held in honor.'

And Michal daughter of Saul had no children to the day of her death."[3]

What a speech David gives to his wife. *"**I will** celebrate before the LORD. **I will** become even more undignified than this, and **I will** be humiliated in my own eyes. But by these slave girls you spoke of, I will be held in honor."* If that is not a "drop the mic" moment, I don't know what is.

Again, I ask, what does your worship do to those around you? Or should I ask, does it do anything to those around you? David clearly did not care what his wife thought, because he understood that his worship was to and for the Lord. The effect it had on those around him was absolutely secondary, but it still affected those around him.

It is important to note it was Michal's pride that kept her from seeing the beauty of David's worship to God, and it was also Michal's pride that brought a curse from heaven upon her.

What is your excuse for not being willing to display your worship before God? Is it pride? Only you and God know the answer to that question.

I have had people "raise their eyebrows," maybe even offer a subtle scowl when I have worshipped in abandonment to God. Sometimes, in those moments, I want to shrink back. But then I remember David's story, and it inspires me to worship with even more passion. My worship is to Him, and my desire is to seek His approval, not the approval of those around me.

When we come into the house of God with the express purpose of exalting Him and giving Him glory with all that we have—with all our hearts—not only will God be pleased, but others will follow suit when they see your pure abandonment to God.

Matthew 2:1-2

"After Jesus was born in Bethlehem in Judea, during the time of King Herod, Magi from the east came to Jerusalem and asked, "Where is the one who has been born king of the Jews?" We saw his star when it rose and have come to worship him."

WORSHIP: "to do reverence to; to worship."[1]

CHAPTER 7

WHAT SHOULD WORSHIP LOOK LIKE?

So what is all the big hoopla about worship anyway? Why can't we just go to church, sing a few cozy songs, listen to a decent sermon, throw 20 bucks in the offering and call it a Sunday? One answer to that is really quite simple: God hates religious routine, and that is exactly what a lot of Christian churches look like today. We have our routine, but after it is all said and done, the Spirit of God is nowhere to be found.

I don't know about you, but I have better things to do with my time than just fulfill a religious duty. If I'm going to church, I want an encounter with God. Otherwise, I might as well stay home and watch Netflix. And yes, I can encounter God on my own, in my home, or even walking along a path with my dog, but there is no replacement for the corporate gathering, where voices are lifted towards heaven and God comes into the center of it.

I believe our worship times should be a reflection of Revelation 4:9-11:

> *"Whenever the living creatures give glory, honor and thanks to him who sits on the throne and who lives for ever and ever, the twenty-four elders fall down before him who sits on the throne and worship him who lives for ever and ever. They lay their crowns before the throne and say:*
>
> *'You are worthy, our Lord and God, to receive glory and honor and power, for you created all things, and by your will they were created and have their being.'"*

I'm fascinated by this image of the elders falling down before the throne and laying their crowns down. The word "lay" is the Greek word "ballō," which is a verb—an action word. Its meanings include "to throw, to cast, to put down, to rush down."[2] One biblical dictionary says it actually means to "hurl," or to "let fall."[3]

To me this means that there should be some action happening when we worship God.

What's really interesting about this is that it appears King David had insight into this whole concept. A brief example of this is in Psalm 28:6-7:

> *"Praise be to the LORD, for he has heard my cry for mercy. The LORD is my strength and my shield; my heart trusts in him, and he helps me. My heart leaps for joy, and with my song I praise him."*

The first "praise" word in this passage is a Hebrew word which translates as *"to bless, to praise, filled with strength, to celebrate, to adore, to bless another,"* [4, 5] and so on. However, the second "praise" word in this passage is a different Hebrew word altogether, which coincidently means "to confess, to throw, to cast." [6] It has some of the same definition as the word "lay" from the book of Revelation.

David is saying that he would bless, celebrate, and adore God because of His great mercy. His heart leaps for joy, and He will throw and cast down with singing. But what is David casting down? Could it be that David is casting his crown down, just like the elders in the book of Revelation? After all, he is a King.

When David dances before the Lord in front of all Israel in 2 Samuel 6:16, he is wearing only a linen ephod. What had he done with his crown?

So what about you and me? Although there are many days when I feel I *deserve* a crown, I don't actually have one. Or do I?

Back in my Bible college days, one of my professors said something that has impacted me to this day. We were in discussion about how to receive praise and compliments, and what to do about it when someone comes up to you and tells you how great or wonderful they think you are. She said the best thing to do is to pretend that each complement is a trophy or a crown. You simply say "thank-you" and receive it. No need for abasement and false humility. Then, she said, at the end of the day or week, get on your knees before the Lord, lay your crowns down, and give them to God. After all, he is the one who made you and gave you your gifts and abilities anyway, so really, all the trophies and crowns belong to him.

What I didn't realize is that she was describing an aspect of what true praise and worship looks like, similar to what we see in David's worship, similar to what we see in the book of Revelation. It's about giving back to God what really belongs to Him, and that is why we worship!

We all have crowns; whether we take pride in how we keep our home or how well we do our job. Whether we are thrilled with the balance sheet at the end of the week in our business or that our homeschooled child passed a test. Maybe it's that we have cultivated a new relationship or managed to maintain an old one. Perhaps it is the broken-down car that we fixed and is now running, the deal we brokered, the building we framed, the weight that we lifted, the cake we made, the child we reared, or the homeless person we helped.

Whatever our lives look like, we do gather crowns, and it's these, we cast down before the Lord during our praise and worship and say "thank-you" for all you have done through us; for "You are worthy, our Lord and God, to receive glory and honor and power, for you created all things, and by your will they were created and have their being."

We all have something to give back to God. If you can't think of anything, then just give yourself. Our praise and worship should be an active *(remember the verb)* display of thankfulness, joy, and adoration; we should sing with our whole hearts and expend ourselves in giving him the glory He deserves.

Psalm 27:6

"Then my head will be exalted above the enemies who surround me; at his sacred tent I will sacrifice with shouts of joy; I will sing and make music to the LORD."

MUSIC: "to sing, praise, play an instrument"[1]

CHAPTER 8

WORSHIPPING WARRIORS ARISE

All of this leads up to another question that I have grappled with, argued about, exhorted, studied, and preached about: does my worship really make a difference? The answer I have come up with is an unequivocal "yes," "yes," and "yes!"

There are things we know in our heads, and things we know by our spirits. I believe the scriptures show that worship matters, not only to God, but also in our temporal, material world. I admit, however, that I know this more from my spirit than I do with my head.

I also believe that the church is in a season where our worship will matter more and more, as the times change and the generation we are living in becomes more precarious than ever before.

We are all called to worship with our whole hearts and in abandonment to God; however, I also believe certain individuals have a "calling" or "mantle" of worship. I believe there are those who have a "gift" of worship. I'm not talking about the ability to play an instrument or sing and lead worship; I simply mean a God-given gift to shift things in the spirit with worship.

In the Old Testament, one of the twelve sons born to Jacob and Leah, who eventually became part of the twelve tribes of Israel, was the fourth son, named Judah.

> *"She conceived again, and when she gave birth to a son she said, "This time I will praise the LORD." So she named him Judah. Then she stopped having children."²*

The name Judah means "praise." There are people today who have been given this name in the spirit realm. They are the worshipping worriers who are called to go into battle ahead of the army and shift the atmosphere so that spiritual victory can be obtained. They carry a weightiness in the spirit in worship, different than most. I have had the opportunity to have some of these people in my life, some being my very dear friends.

There have been times when I have been asked to lead worship and I have had what felt like the weight of the world on my shoulders. There have been weeks in which everything that could go wrong has, and it seems like every demon in hell has my number. Those were the times I most strongly relied on individuals who carry this special anointing for worship to assist me in the spirit. Often, I don't even communicate how I'm feeling verbally, but as soon as these worshippers begin, it's like they push back the heaviness in the spiritual realm and a huge weight comes off me, and I can then, push in and lead like I need to.

Too many people take this call to worship lightly. They assume that if they are not in the mood, or if they so choose, they can just walk away from their worship mandate. But what they don't realize is that they are leaving a huge hole in the spiritual armor that someone else has to fill! It's kind of like leaving the ranks of the army in the heat of battle, because you suddenly feel like being somewhere else. Not only would that be ludicrous, but it would also be very dangerous.

I know of some key worship warriors who have laid down their weapons of worship and left the scene—or may have never entered the scene. Their reasons vary. Some are tired, wounded, and disillusioned; some are just being selfish, childish, and wanting their own way. Some are just too lazy to put the energy into it; some are walking in fear; some are walking in unforgiveness and resentment; others would rather listen to the lie of the enemy than to the Spirit of God. Whatever the reason, I know that not only does this hurt God, it also saddens my heart as well. It also puts a greater weight on those who are still contending and being faithful in worship for the things of God. The church needs the "Judahs," the warriors, to step up and take their place.

I'm well aware there are times when life takes its toll on us. We get worn out and maybe even disillusioned with worship and the things around us. Believe me, I have had seasons in my life when all I want to do is quit and go home. But every time I begin to feel that way, I am reminded of the scripture which exhorts me, even commands me to "*not become weary in doing good, for at the proper time we will reap a harvest if we do not give up.*"³

Weariness seems unavoidable at times, but quitting or giving up is absolutely a choice and should NEVER be an option. The Apostle Paul teaches in the book of Ephesians that when the battles rage and you have done all you can, you are to stand your ground.

"...Finally, be strong in the Lord and in his mighty power. Put on the full armor of God, so that you can take your stand against the devil's schemes. For our struggle is not against flesh and blood, but against the rulers, against the authorities, against the powers of this dark world and against the spiritual forces of evil in the heavenly realms. Therefore put on the full armor of God, so that when the day of evil comes, you may be able to stand your ground, and after you have done everything, to stand"[4]

Even if you feel like you aren't moving ahead in the spirit, quitting is still not an option. It's time for the worshipping warriors to get back into the fight.

I believe certain strongholds in the spirit realm can only be pushed back by the sound of praise and worship. The devil, who hates us, also hates it when we give praise and worship to God. It is the thing that the devil longs to possess (read the book of Revelation if you have any doubts). He wanted the worship of man, and he wants your worship now. Lucifer the archangel of worship, now fallen, understands the power of worship and praise. We as a church cannot stay in a place of ignorance and complacency. We need to understand the purpose and power of worship as well. We need to know how it plays a role in what the church is called to accomplish in our world today.

Francis Frangipane says this in his article titled "Army of Worshipers":

> "When the Scriptures refer to the "heavenly host," we usually think of "choirs of angels." The word "host" in the Bible meant "army" (Joshua 5:13-14). It is an important truth: the hosts of Heaven are worshiping armies. Indeed, no one can do warfare who is not first a worshiper of God."[5]

Worship is all of the things described in this book: it is bowing in reverence, casting our crowns, and shouting with joy, but it is also a weapon for use against the devil. We are all called to be a spiritual army of worshippers who push back the powers of darkness. An army is of little use without its generals and commanders. This is the call of those who are gifted in worship. This is not a season in which the warriors can lay aside their weapons of worship and pretend like it doesn't matter. It matters more than we know.

Worshipping warriors arise!

John 9:37-38

"Jesus said, 'You have now seen him; in fact, he is the one speaking with you.' Then the man said, 'Lord, I believe,' and he worshiped him."

WORSHIP: "worship; bow down; kneel down"[1]

CHAPTER 9

LIAR, LIAR

Jim Carrey starred in a movie a while back called *Liar, Liar*. It was a comedy about a man who was a lawyer and basically lied for a living. (Note: I love the law and do not believe that lawyers are liars.) In this movie, the man's son makes a birthday wish and suddenly this lawyer cannot tell a lie for a whole day. This of course wreaks havoc in the poor man's life for the next 24 hours. The movie is fun to watch and has a nice, happy ending. This critic gives it two thumbs up.

I once had a friend who was very emotionally committed to me. She was my greatest, most passionate defender and promoter. At times, it felt like I could do no wrong in her eyes. That is, until we had a misunderstanding and she felt that I had lied to her. I still remember the wounded venom that came out of her when she confronted me and stated that I had lied to her and she could never forgive me. With the same passion with which she had defended me, she now railed against me. Even after I clarified the situation, I believe she never really got over it.

What is it about lying that can tear friendships apart, cause children to despise their parents, end a marriage forever, and cause unbelievable pain and consequences? Even God Almighty made lying a violation of his commands in the book of Genesis. So what's my point? What about when we tell lies in worship? Have you ever thought about this? I have…more than you know.

I remember as a teenager being convicted about this very thing. As I said, I was raised in church and we used to sing an old chorus called, "I Have Decided to Follow Jesus." It was very popular in its day, and yet the last line of each "stanza" used to bother me because it said, *"no turning back, no turning back."*[2] Sometimes when we would get to that line of the song, I would simply hum the melody because I didn't want to make any declarations that I might not keep.

Or how about the song *Lord I Give You My Heart*? That has some serious lines in it, such as:

> *"Lord I give you my heart,*
> *I give you my soul, I live for you alone.*

Every breath that I take,
Every moment I'm awake,
Have your way in me."[3]

It's great until you get to the line "*I live for you alone.*" Do you really live for Him alone? I've witnessed personal friends and family sing this song and then commit blatant sin the very next day. What happened to living for God alone? This is a serious declaration.

Sometimes after watching people worship, I almost want to laugh. It's sadly amusing to watch someone sing lyrics such as, "*With Everything! With Everything! I shout for your glory; With Everything! With Everything! We will shout forth Your Praise*"[4] while they are sitting down, countenance fallen, shoulders sloped, clearly not at all engaged in what is happening in the room.

I wonder if this matters to God.

> "*But I say unto you, that every idle word that men shall speak, they shall give account thereof in the day of judgment.*"[5]

I know what I think when I read this scripture, but put this verse in context and decide what you think for yourself. I often wonder if we will have to give an account of what we speak or sing in worship when our heart is not there at all. Are these idle words? A brief definition of idle is: "lazy, useless, without thought, indifferent."[6]

I absolutely believe God is full of grace, and I do not live in fear of the lover of my soul. But I do believe we need a higher standard in our heart of worship than what we have. How can we can sit on our hands, yawn, stretch, and barely open our mouth as we sing lyrics such as *"Everything inside me wants more of you."*[7]

Liar, liar?

Psalm 52:8-9

*"But I am like an olive tree flourishing in the house of
God; I trust in God's unfailing love for ever and ever.
For what you have done I will always praise you in the
presence of your faithful people. And I will hope in your
name, for your name is good."*

PRAISE: "to throw, to cast, to confess, to take
confession, to give thanks, to praise,
to celebrate, give voice."[1]

CHAPTER 10

WORSHIP WHEN IT HURTS

"David noticed that his attendants were whispering among themselves, and he realized the child was dead. "Is the child dead?" he asked.

"Yes," they replied, "he is dead."

Then David got up from the ground. After he had washed, put on lotions and changed his clothes, he went into the house of the LORD and worshiped."[2]

Have you ever had something tragic happen in your life or to those close to you? Do you have any regrets in life? Have you ever done something and then wished you could go back in time, even just for a few seconds, and re-do the whole thing?

I'm sure there are very few of us who have *"no regrets"* in life. I like what Forest Gump says: "stupid is as stupid does." I'm sure most of us have done some stupid things in life.

I love the story of David in 2 Samuel 12. David messed up big time, and many of us would have written him off for sure, especially since he was king. We wonder how he dared to be so selfish.

What I love about this story is that even though David thought he got away with all his sins, God called him out, and then showed such incredibly great mercy.

That is how God is. He will chastise and put us in our place, but He is always full of grace and mercy.

I love David's response to God's discipline. God tells David that his child will die as a consequence for the sin he committed. David, rather than being angry at God, goes into a time of fasting and prayer for the child. Through his relationship with God, David hopes that maybe he can change God's mind about letting the child live. When the child finally dies, and David hears about it, he does something that most of us would never even consider doing. He gets up, gets cleaned up, and then goes to the house of the Lord to worship!

Now let's be real. If someone told me that a loved one of mine had just died, the last thing I would want to do is to get dressed and leave my house. Most of us would curl up in a ball and hide in our beds for a week or so. Then, maybe we would consider taking a shower. But going to the house of the Lord to worship? Why would David do that?

I believe the answer to the question is in the definition of worship. If you look at the Hebrew word "worship", in this context, it literally means *"to bow oneself down, to sink down, to depress, **to submit oneself.**"*[3] I believe this is what David was doing in this situation. He was submitting himself to the will of God.

David worshipped the Lord by submitting himself to God, even when it was difficult for him. Even though David did not like God's will at that moment, he understood who God was. David understood that even though he was *a* King, he knew that God was *the* King of Kings! He understood authority, supremacy, and submission, and it was important for him to demonstrate this, not only to others around him but to God himself. He was submitted to God's authority and will, even when it hurt.

Another demonstration of this type of worship in scripture is in the story of Abraham and his son Isaac.

"Some time later God tested Abraham. He said to him, 'Abraham!'

'Here I am,' he replied.

Then God said, 'Take your son, your only son, whom you love—Isaac—and go to the region of Moriah. Sacrifice him there as a burnt offering on a mountain I will show you.'

Early the next morning Abraham got up and loaded his donkey. He took with him two of his servants and his son Isaac. When he had cut enough wood for the burnt offering, he set out for the place God had told him about. On the third day Abraham looked up and saw the place in the distance. He said to his servants, 'Stay here with the donkey while I and the boy go over there. We will worship and then we will come back to you.'"4

Here again, we see worship happening in a most difficult and unbelievable situation. God was asking Abraham for everything. Abraham and Sarah had longed for this child all of their married lives, and finally when they are at that place of enjoying their child, God asks them for the ultimate sacrifice. As a parent, I can't even imagine what this must have been like for Abraham. Yet, we see that Abraham worshiped

God by submitted himself to God's will and was willing to sacrifice his only child because he understood the supremacy of God.

Again, this is such an amazing picture of true worship. Too many of us have decided we can only worship when things are just right. We worship because God has blessed us, and we worship because we have all that we need. We worship because the music suits us and inspires us, or when we are feeling good and rested and have time in our busy schedules. We worship when the birds are singing, and joy is flooding our hearts. But what about when the opposite is true?

Can you still worship when things suck? Can you worship when God has not answered your prayers? Can you worship when the kids are sick, or when someone has hurt you? Can you worship when everything seems to be falling apart around you, and when there is no money in the bank? Can you worship when you don't feel like it or when you "just feel out of sorts"? Can you still bow down and give him reverence even when it seems God has been unfair to you? Can you still worship when the prophetic word he declared over you has not come true, or His promises to you have not yet been fulfilled? Can you worship in submission to His will even when you don't want to? True worship is when we can submit our will to the will of God, even when we think He should have done something differently.

I have seen some very learned and intelligent people unable to grasp this simple principle: that worship is not about us—it's about Him, the King of Kings and Lord of Lords! It's about His will and purposes, not yours or mine. If we could only grasp this, we would be so much further ahead in our spiritual lives instead of being stuck in the same place that we were last year this time.

David submitted to God's will even though it must have been horribly painful for him. Even though his son has just died, he worships and eventually brings the legacy of Solomon into the world, one of the greatest men of all time. God's ways are not our ways, He is Lord; we are not.

I have a dear friend who is called to be one of those worshipping warriors I mentioned in a previous chapter. Even when she was new to the Lord and the things of God, it seemed she had an immediate understanding in her heart of what worship was for. She was completely naive about the things of God, but she had that mantle of worship I talked about. Her worship, through flagging, could shift the atmosphere in the whole room in a moment.

One of the most impacting things I remember about her occurred when her father passed away. I was told early that Saturday afternoon that her dad had died. My heart went out to her, and I admit that I was worried that this tragedy might knock her off the path of her pursuit of God. To my surprise, this young woman came to church a bit late that Saturday night (which is when we have church) and went straight to the front, picked up some flags, and worshipped with all of her might. It still moves me when I think of that time so many years ago. She had the key of David, even though she didn't know it or understand it.

This may sound strange to some, but I believe worship should always cost us something. In these stories, with what had just happened; David, Abraham, and my friend's worship cost them something, it cost them their wills, submitted to God's will. I dream that our worship would always be so acceptable and pleasing to God.

Revelation 4:9-11

"Whenever the living creatures give glory, honor and thanks to him who sits on the throne and who lives for ever and ever, the twenty-four elders fall down before him who sits on the throne and worship him who lives for ever and ever. They lay their crown before the throne and say: 'You are worthy, our Lord and God, to receive glory and honor and power, for you created all things, and by your will they were created and have their being.'"

WORSHIP: "prostrate oneself before."[1]

CHAPTER 11

WHY I WORSHIP

One of the greatest lessons my father taught me is that life is not all about me. Throughout my life, at different times, he would remind me of this simple truth. Whether it was when my brother and I had to give up our bedrooms and bunk on the floor so that someone could stay at our house for a day…or six months. Whether, we had to give up our seat at the table to show honor to someone else at dinner time. Whether we had to shovel the neighbor's driveway because they were ill, and we had health. These little lessons spoke loudly and clearly: I was not as important as I thought I was at the time.

I think one of the greatest tragedies in parenting today is we have given our children a sense of entitlement. We have made them the center of their lives, rather than teaching them life is not all about them. But I digress—perhaps that will be another book.

I'm so very grateful for this lesson because it has made my life, and indeed my understanding of worship, so much easier to grasp. I know, without any difficulty at all, that my worship is not about me. I understand that the purpose of worship is not for me, even though I benefit so greatly from it. I understand it is the sacrifice of praise and worship, my heart and soul focused on Him and not on me; that makes my worship pleasing to God. I worship because He is Lord and I am not.

Some would say that this is not as great a revelation as I make it out to be, but I beg to differ. It is one of the greatest revelations of all! I know this because I have seen for more than forty years, and continue to see, people who love God, unable to worship because they are so focused on themselves they are blinded to anything else.

One of my favorite songs of late is called "King of My Heart" written by John Mark & Sarah McMillan:

> *"Let the King of my heart*
> *Be the mountain where I run,*
> *The fountain I drink from…He is my song.*
> *Let the King of my heart*

Be the shadow where I hide,
The ransom for my life…He is my song.
Let the King of my heart
Be the wind inside my sails,
The anchor in the waves…He is my song.
Let the King of my heart
Be the fire inside my veins,
The echo of my days…He is my song."[2]

The very title of the song is significant: "King of my Heart." So many have not made Him king of their hearts. Indeed many are saved and have asked Jesus into their hearts, but many do not understand the principle of kingship and lordship. Too many of us are driven by the feelings of our heart, and we allow life and circumstance to dictate whether or not we should, will, or want to worship. Yet, when we grasp the fact that worship is about God, who is good *all the time,* no matter what our circumstances, it changes our ability to worship. When we understand that yes, there is a residual benefit for ourselves when we worship; but that the purpose is to exalt Him in all of His goodness, then circumstances and feelings become irrelevant. He indeed is good!

When I worship, I feel a supernatural alignment that comes into my spirit which puts things in perspective. My heart and mind become aligned with heaven. At times, I have had to lead worship when I have been upset with my husband, disappointed in a friend, saddened by a circumstance, had a sick child in the hospital, have been "feeling under the weather," or been under straight-up demonic attack. My emotional preference would be to stay home, or at the very least relinquish my responsibility to someone else and just sit in the congregation.

However, I have found that it is in those times when it is most difficult, I have the deepest worship. When I focus on the truths that He is good, He is Alpha and Omega, King of Kings and Lord of Lords, He is mighty, omniscient, and He is worthy of it all, suddenly something changes in my heart. I feel the presence of God come, sometimes with such force that I begin to weep. I want only to fall on my knees, cast my crowns down, and sing, "Holy, Holy, Holy is the Lord God Almighty!"

One of these times occurred when one of my twin boys was sick with the croup. The boys were two years old, and we had planned a worship event with the churches in our community. This event was directed by God, and we knew that God wanted to meet us in a unique way because of the unity that was happening in the churches. Of course, the enemy was angry and tried to wreak havoc in many different ways. My son Jesse got so sick with croup that he ended up in the hospital days before the event.

I had been scheduled to do worship for part of the event, and I remember sitting inside Jesse's croup tent, exhausted from holding him as he struggled to breathe, and thinking "God, this is not fair. How can I leave my baby and go lead worship?" I was confused and a bit angry. I did not want to go; but I felt the Spirit of God whisper to me, "Go." I asked the nurse to watch him, and even though I was somewhat annoyed with the whole situation, I went to the church.

The event had already started, so I walked in and went to the piano. I began to lead the songs as requested. As I did, a crazy anointing came upon me. I remember what felt like a bolt of energy shoot through me. I began to prophesy and serve notice to the enemy that we would not stop—that the purposes of God would be established. I don't remember all that I spoke because it was completely under the unction of Holy Spirit. After I finished leading the songs I was supposed to lead, I left the platform, and went right back to the hospital. Jesse came home the next morning, completely fine.

It makes me so sad when I see people who either do not or cannot connect with God because of a misunderstanding of what worship is supposed to be. The church "worship" service for them is just filling time, a ritual or a duty at best. So many miss the opportunity to "touch the hem of His garment," so to speak, to be healed, restored, renewed, and have their hearts set free, all because they do not know that worship is for Him.

It is in the difficult times, when my praise starts out as a sacrifice, that His presence comes. He is pleased that I understand the purpose of worship. It is then that He walks into the room and pours out over me his grace, mercy, and strength. It is in those moments that revelation is renewed in my heart and mind, and I begin to feel invigorated to know that God Almighty, the Lord of the universe, sees my worship. I feel honored that He has chosen me to war in the spirit with my worship; that He has called me to raise up a standard; it is then that I walk away from it fulfilled, blessed, and longing for more.

That is why I worship.

Psalm 57:7-11

"My heart, O God, is steadfast, my heart is steadfast; I will sing and make music. Awake, my soul! Awake, harp and lyre! I will awaken the dawn. I will praise you, Lord, among the nations; I will sing of you among the peoples. For great is your love, reaching to the heavens; your faithfulness reaches to the skies. Be exalted, O God, above the heavens; let your glory be over all the earth."

PRAISE: "to throw, to cast, to profess, to confess, to show, to give thanks, to praise, to celebrate, to praise the name of Jehovah"[1]

CONCLUSION

Fourteen years ago, my husband and I planted our first church. We were young, raw, and inexperienced, and we knew it, but we didn't care. We knew we had to do what we were called to do, and part of our mandate was to be worshippers.

There were times in our worship services that the floor of the little Presbyterian Church we were renting would literally move to the rhythm of the dancer's feet as we jumped and danced in worship. On one occasion, we had to tell our people to "dial it down a bit" because the grand piano was lifting off the floor with each pulse of the music. We were radical in worship, and we had such amazing times of connecting with the presence of God.

One time just after the worship, one of our newest coverts went outside for a cigarette. She quickly came back in and yelled, "Hey everyone, come look outside!" We all exited the church while our guest speaker was on the platform, and in the sky was the most amazing display of God's handiwork. What looked like rainbows were shooting straight up from the mountains into the skies, surrounded by clouds that were moving and forming crazy shapes and colours.

The sky appeared to be divided into three sections. One section of the sky was blood red with a wild lightning storm in the background. (You could almost see the spiritual battle happening in the heavenlies.) Another section of the sky had an intensely golden sunset-colored cloud display going on. The third section of sky had a beautiful blue hue to it. It was so powerful! You could feel such a strong tangible presence of God in the air.

Some of our people ran back into the church, grabbed their flags and began flagging outside on the lawn. Some were yelling at the top of their lungs, while others were laughing and dancing. My husband and one of our young people climbed on top of the church roof. My husband began blowing the shofar and yelling into the air, as we all gave God glory in praise.

The funny part of this story is that the church building we were renting at the time was located right at the intersection of one of the major streets in town. So, you can image the chaos this scene generated. People who were driving by began to slow down to see what was happening. Some even pulled over and were looking to see what it was that we were so excited about. You could see the confusion on their faces as they saw these wild church people outside of the church, worshipping and praising God as they basked in the manifest glory of His presence!

Of course, living in a small town, rumors began to spread about our crazy little church; some began calling it a cult, while others called it a glorified youth group. Still others were not sure how to define it. But like someone once said, if the world is not talking about your church maybe it's because your church has become irrelevant.

I tell this story because I believe it is a small picture of what the church, in worship, should look like and accomplish. Our worship should generate such a response from heaven that it causes the manifest glory of God to be seen not only by those who desire it, but also by an unbelieving world. God wants to show up in our worship!

Let's face it, we live in a day when things around us are changing rapidly. Whether it's political upsets, crazy weather patterns, social transitions, or technological advances, nothing is like it used to be. There is coming a day, which is soon to be upon us, when the world will be looking for answers amid the confusion. It is in this season that the church will have the opportunity to rise to the occasion and become a relevant and sought-out source of reassurance and hope. One of the keys is that the church must re-focus its heart towards God in worship.

A narcissistic mentality from the world has seeped into the church and into our worship—the idea that worship is all about me. When this happens, it emasculates the church because we have our focus in the wrong place.

As I look at the stories in the Old Testament, I can see this same tendency in the children of Israel. God wanted them, as His chosen ones, to be a representation of how God loves. He desired for them to be well fed and cared for. As they simply looked to Him, He would fight their battles, He would give them homes they did not build; they would eat from fields they did not plant, and they were to multiply and influence every nation around them.

They were to have no cares and no concerns, if only they would worship the one true God. When they focused on God, He would focus on them. Yet, we can see that the children of Israel struggled with this mandate and often allowed mixture to come into their hearts. They would end up worshipping other gods, which always brought them to a place of destruction and ruin. Only when they would repent, turn their hearts back to God and "worship Him only" would things begin to turn around.

I dare say, I see some of the same happening in our churches today. We have succumbed to the same syndrome that the children of Israel did. We have turned our hearts to other gods, and one of those gods is ourselves.

It's time for us as believers to re-focus. It is time for us to set our affections back towards God. One of the ways to do this is through worship. I reiterate that worship is an everyday experience. It's offering our bodies as living sacrifices in all that we do. It's not just about singing and music in a church setting, but it absolutely does include this. The scriptures exhort us in Hebrews 10:24-25, saying:

> *"And let us consider how we may spur one another on toward love and good deeds, not giving up meeting together, as some are in the habit of doing, but encouraging one another--and all the more as you see the day approaching."*

Our corporate gatherings are needed! They help us stay connected in the business of life, and it is in these times that we can corporately give our praises to God, worshipping him in unity. It is in this setting that we can exhort and encourage each other towards God. It is in this place that we can bring our crowns and lay them at His feet. It is in this atmosphere that we can humble ourselves before Him and each other, showing our adoration to Him. It is in these moments that we can inspire each other to worship with even more passion. It is at these times that our corporate praise and worship will catch the attention of heaven and a new release of His glory will come.

Maybe it won't look like the scene I described of our church in the early days, but then again, maybe it will. Wouldn't it be amazing to literally see in the heavens an open display of God's glory over his people as we worship Him? It happened before, and it can happen again. I believe God wants it to happen, and He's waiting for us to get re-aligned.

He gave us a taste back then and it's what I crave now. Can you imagine the attraction and effect this would have on the world around us? Can you envision the sudden relevance the church would have in a hurting and dying world? This is what I yearn for; this is the hunger that drives me in worship. I long to see His glory displayed as it was in the temple when the priests could not perform their duties; to see an open display of His glory in the skies as we did in the early days of our church. Oh that we would worship in such a way that

God could not resist but to come and dwell amongst us like never before.

May this be the answer to the question, "why worship?"

ABOUT THE AUTHOR

Heather Lucier is a pastor, musician, worship leader, itinerant minister, wife, and mother from Kitimat, British Columbia, Canada.

Worship has been a part of Heather's life for years. With experience comes her unique, honest, and somewhat humorous perspective regarding the topics of worship, worship leading, and the call to the body of Christ regarding worship today. She shares her passion for music through teaching and training up those called to music ministry and worship.

Heather and her husband Art have pastored *The Harvest Church* in Kitimat since 2003. They also work and serve with *Be a Hero Canada* and *Breakthrough Ministries* out of Kelowna, BC. They are also in the process of planting churches in the northern regions of British Columbia.

They have a heart for the First Peoples and travel and minister in villages across western Canada, bringing a fresh sound of worship and a message of hope and restoration.

ReviverMinistries.com

ABOUT REVIVER MINISTRIES

ITINERANT MINISTRY:

Both Heather and Art minister publicly in the areas of worship leading, teaching, and preaching. They travel with their band, Reviver, which is known for a passionate, zealous flare for worship. To book an engagement please email ReviverMinistries@gmail. com, or visit our website at ReviverMinistries.com.

WORSHIP CDS:

Visit our website to check out Reviver's two worship CDs.

"Deep & Dance" – includes worship songs written and recorded by Art Lucier.

"Forgiven" – recorded live in Kelowna, BC after the Journey of Freedom in 2010, featuring worship with the First Nations' "Abba" drum.

ENDNOTES

INTRODUCTION

1. Gesenius, Friedrich Wilhelm. *Gesenius' Hebrew-Chaldee Lexicon to the Old Testament.* Baker Book House Company, 1979.

CHAPTER 1

1. Holladay, William L. *A Concise Hebrew and Aramaic Lexicon of the Old Testament*, WM.B. Eerdmans Publishing Co., 1971.

2. Gesenius, Friedrich Wilhelm. *Gesenius' Hebrew-Chaldee Lexicon to the Old Testament.* Baker Book House Company, 1979.

CHAPTER 2

1. Gesenius, Friedrich Wilhelm. *Gesenius' Hebrew-Chaldee Lexicon to the Old Testament.* Baker Book House Company, 1979.

CHAPTER 3

1. Swanson, James. *A Dictionary of Biblical Languages with Semantic Domains: Greek (New Testament).* Faithlife, 1997.

CHAPTER 4

1. Gesenius, Friedrich Wilhelm. *Gesenius' Hebrew-Chaldee Lexicon to the Old Testament.* Baker Book House Company, 1979.

2. Mangum Douglas, Derek R. Brown, Rachel Klippenstein, and Rebekah Hurst. *Lexham Theological Wordbook-Logos Bible Software.* Lexham Press Books, 2014.

3. Mangum Douglas, Derek R. Brown, Rachel Klippenstein, and Rebekah Hurst. *Lexham Theological Wordbook-Logos Bible Software.* Lexham Press Books, 2014.

4. Mangum Douglas, Derek R. Brown, Rachel Klippenstein, and Rebekah Hurst. *Lexham Theological Wordbook-Logos Bible Software.* Lexham Press Books, 2014.

5. Spicq, Ceslas, and James Ernest. *Theological Lexicon of the New Testament.* Hendrickson, 1994.

6. John 4:21-24 (AMP)

CHAPTER 5

1. Strong, James. *The New Strong's Concise Dictionary of Bible Words.* Faithlife, 2009.

CHAPTER 6

1. Gesenius, Friedrich Wilhelm. *Gesenius' Hebrew-Chaldee Lexicon to the Old Testament.* Baker Book House Company, 1979.

2. 2 Samuel 6:15

3. 2 Samuel 6:16, 20-23

CHAPTER 7

1. *The Lexham Analytical Lexicon to the Greek New Testament.* Lexham Press, 2011.

2. *The Lexham Analytical Lexicon to the Greek New Testament.* Lexham Press, 2011.

3. Swanson, James. *A Dictionary of Biblical Languages with Semantic Domains: Greek (New Testament).* Faithlife, 1997.

4. Strong, James. *The New Strong's Concise Dictionary of Bible Words:* Faithlife 2009.

5. Gesenius, Friedrich Wilhelm. *Gesenius' Hebrew-Chaldee Lexicon to the Old Testament.* Baker Book House Company, 1979.

6. Gesenius, Friedrich Wilhelm. *Gesenius' Hebrew-Chaldee Lexicon to the Old Testament.* Baker Book House Company, 1979.

CHAPTER 8

1. Strong, James. *The New Strong's Concise Dictionary of Bible Words:* Faithlife 2009.

2. Genesis 29:35

3. Galatians 6:9

4. Ephesians 6:10-13

5. Frangipane, Francis. "Army of Worshippers." *The Elijah List,* 4 April 2012. www.elijahlist.com/words/display_word. html?ID=10882. Accessed 3 October 2017.

CHAPTER 9

1. *The Lexham Analytical Lexicon to the Greek New Testament.* Lexham Press, 2011.

2. Singh, Sadhu Sundar. "I Have Decided to Follow Jesus." *Timeless Truths Free Online Library*, www.library. timelesstruths.org/music/I_Have_Decided_to_Follow_ Jesus/ Accessed 3 October 2017.

3. Hillsong Worship. "I Give You My Heart." Composed by Reuben Morgan. *God Is in the House.* Hillsong Music Publishing, 1996.

4. Hillsong Worship. "With Everything." *This Is Our God,* Hillsong Music Publishing, 2008.

5. Matthew 12:36 (KJV)

6. Swanson, James. *A Dictionary of Biblical Languages with Semantic Domains: Greek (New Testament).* Faithlife, 1997.

7. Smith, Dustin. "Everything Inside Me." *Live from World Revival Church,* Rushing Waters, 2013.

CHAPTER 10

1. Gesenius, Friedrich Wilhelm. *Gesenius' Hebrew-Chaldee*

Lexicon to the Old Testament. Baker Book House Company, 1979.

2. 2 Samuel 12:19-20

3. Gesenius, Friedrich Wilhelm. *Gesenius' Hebrew-Chaldee Lexicon to the Old Testament.* Baker Book House Company, 1979.

4. Genesis 22:1-5

CHAPTER 11

1. Swanson, James. *A Dictionary of Biblical Languages with Semantic Domains: Greek (New Testament).* Faithlife, 1997.

2. McMillan, John Mark and Sarah. "King of My Heart." *You Are the Avalanche.* Capitol Christian Music Group, 2015.

Conclusion

1. Gesenius, Friedrich Wilhelm. *Gesenius' Hebrew-Chaldee Lexicon to the Old Testament.* Baker Book House Company, 1979.

WORKS CITED

The Bible. The Amplified Bible. The Lockman Foundation, 1987.

The Bible. King James Version. Hendrickson, 2006.

The Bible. The NIV Study Bible, 10th Anniversary Edition. Zondervan, 1995.

The Bible. New Living Translation. Tyndale House, 2015

Frangipane, Francis. "Army of Worshippers." *The Elijah List,* 4 April 2012. www.elijahlist.com/words/display_word. html?ID=10882. Accessed 3 October 2017.

Gesenius, Friedrich Wilhelm. *Gesenius' Hebrew-Chaldee Lexicon to the Old Testament*. Baker Book House Company, 1979.

Hillsong Worship. "I Give You My Heart." Composed by Reuben Morgan. *God Is in the House*. Hillsong Music Publishing, 1996.

Hillsong Worship. "With Everything." *This Is Our God,* Hillsong Music Publishing, 2008.

Holladay, William L. *A Concise Hebrew and Aramaic Lexicon of the Old Testament*. WM.B. Eerdmans Publishing Co., 1971.

The Lexham Analytical Lexicon to the Greek New Testament. Lexham Press, 2011.

Mangum Douglas, Derek R. Brown, Rachel Klippenstein, and Rebekah Hurst. *Lexham Theological Wordbook-Logos Bible Software*. Lexham Press Books, 2014.

McMillan, John Mark and Sarah. "King of My Heart." *You Are the Avalanche*. Capitol Christian Music Group, 2015.

Singh, Sadhu Sundar. "I Have Decided to Follow Jesus." *Timeless Truths Free Online Library*, www.library.timelesstruths.org/music/I_Have_Decided_to_Follow_Jesus/ Accessed 3 October 2017.

Smith, Dustin. "Everything Inside Me." *Live from World Revival Church,* Rushing Waters, 2013.

Spicq, Ceslas and James Ernest. *Theological Lexicon of the New Testament*. Hendrickson, 1994.

Strong, James. *The New Strong's Concise Dictionary of Bible Words:* Faithlife, 2009.

Swanson, James. *A Dictionary of Biblical Languages with Semantic Domains: Greek (New Testament)*. Faithlife, 1997.

All scriptures are taken from the New International Version of the Bible unless otherwise noted.